COQUI

¡Hola! Hello!

Written by Valery Ortiz
Illustrated by Adrienne Lovette

COQUÍ
Text copyright ©2011 by Valery Ortiz
Illutstration copyright ©2019 by Adrienne Lovette

All rights reserved. This book may not be reproduced in any form,
in whole or in part (beyond the copying permitted by US Copyright Law,
Section 107, "fair use" in teaching or research, Section 108,
ceratin library copying, or in published media by reviewers in limited
excerpts), without written permission from the author.
For information visit www.HolaHelloSeries.com.

The artists used watercolors and digital techniques to create the digital illustrations
for this book.

I dedicate this book to my parents who proudly kept our traditional Puerto Rican roots alive, and so intently taught me the beauty in being myself.

And to my 10-year-old self, you did it!!!

¡Mi amigo! My friend!
Look closely and you'll find...

I don't "ribbit" like other frogs —
I'm one of a kind!

¡Mi amigo! My friend!
Do you know my song?
If you remember my name,
you can't go wrong —

Coquí

Coquí

Coquí

¡Espera! Wait! My song's different, I know.
It's not what you're used to,
but I hope you don't go!

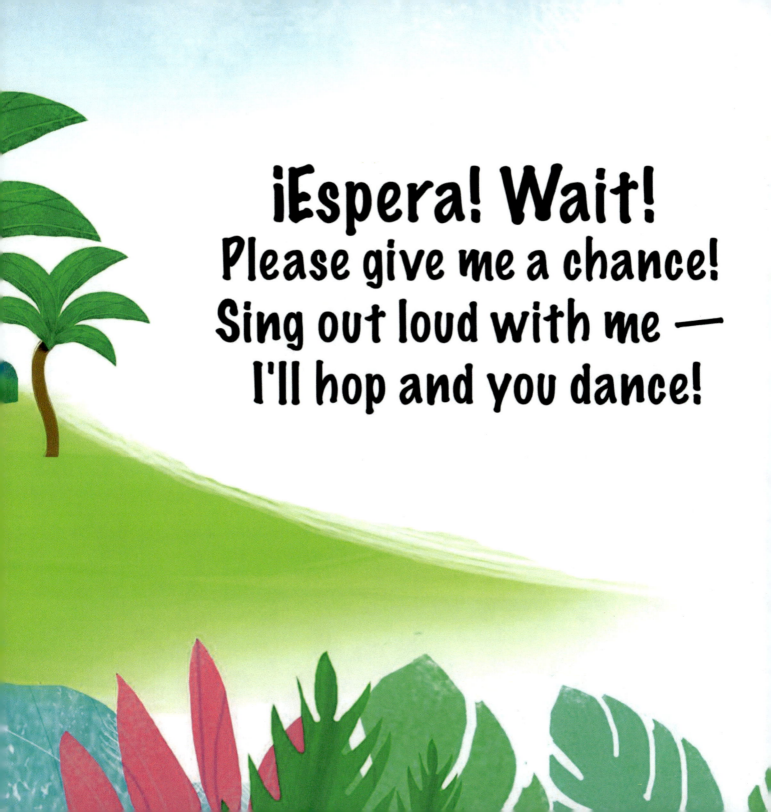

¡Espera! Wait!
Please give me a chance!
Sing out loud with me —
I'll hop and you dance!

Coquí

Coquí

Coquí

¡Que bueno! That's good!
I'm small, don't you see?
But my music is loud,
so you know that it's me!

¡Que bueno! That's good!
I have a new friend.
You didn't care that I don't "ribbit" —
I didn't have to pretend!

¡Gracias! Thank you!
Today I was me!
I'm a tiny tree frog,
my name is Coquí!

¡Adios! Goodbye!
Be yourself, and just play!

And if you ever feel lonely,
I'll show you the way!

Coquí

Coquí

Coquí

VALERY ORTIZ, Author

Valery Ortiz stars as Dina Duran, Gabby's caring and career-driven mom in Disney Channel's unique live action comedy series "Gabby Duran & the Unsittables."

Born in San Juan, Puerto Rico, Ortiz grew up in Orlando, Florida with an early love of dancing and performing that led to roles in local theater productions. After moving to Los Angeles, she continued her acting career playing characters on both the big and small screens, including "Date Movie", "South of Nowhere", "Hit The Floor", "Switched at Birth," "NCIS," "Marvel's Agents of S.H.I.E.L.D.," "Two and a Half Men," "Melissa & Joey," and "Cold Case." In addition, Ortiz previously hosted the "ABC Family Lounge" for the series "Pretty Little Liars," and was the host of "American Latino TV."

Ortiz is also currently pursuing another lifelong dream of publishing her literary works including a collection of poems and a bilingual children's book series called "¡Hola! Hello!"

When not working, Ortiz lends her time to organizations like the Los Angeles Mission, Special Needs Network, Inc. for Autistic Kids, and Best Friends Animal Society.

  @ValeryOrtiz    @OfficialValeryOrtiz

ADRIENNE LOVETTE, Illustrator

Adrienne Lovette is an award-winning director, actor, and writer. She was born in San Juan, Puerto Rico, and grew up in Orlando, Florida. In her early career, she was a director for the Orlando Youth Theatre and academy where she directed children from ages 3 to 18 in various musicals and plays. After moving to New York City, Adrienne created her own indie film company called The Garage Productions, which focuses on people who are diverse and underrepresented. She has directed several award-winning films such as HIDDEN DAYLIGHT, BLIND DATE, THIS BOY'S VIDA and the web-series YOU'RE THE PEST.

As an actor, Adrienne has played opposite Naomi Watts, Aziz Ansari, Joaquin Phoenix, Sam Rockwell, and Michelle Williams. A few of Adrienne's favorite TV roles include BETTER CALL SAUL (AMC), RAY DONOVAN (Showtime), FOSSE/VERDON (FX), THE DEUCE (HBO), THE SINNER (USA), MASTER OF NONE (NETFLIX), MR. ROBOT (USA), and GOTHAM (FOX). She is also known for her role in the feature film, SUNLIGHT JR. (Tribeca Film Festival) playing opposite Naomi Watts.

For more information on her acting and directing, visit her at www.AdrienneLovette.com, www.AnAdrienneLovetteFilm.com, and www.TheGarageProductions.com.

 @AdrienneLovette    @AFLovette

Made in United States
Orlando, FL
03 March 2024

44345119R00020